Labour Loo

Labour
to Israel

Society and p...

Edited by
Paul Kelemen

Foreword by
Ivan Lewis MP

Labour Looks to Israel

Essays on politics, society and peace

Edited by
Paul Richards

Foreword by
Ivan Lewis MP

LABOUR
FRIENDS
of ISRAEL

First published in Great Britain in 2005 by
Labour Friends of Israel
BM LFI
London WC1N 3XX
www.lfi.org.uk
in association with Profile Books Ltd
www.profilebooks.com

Copyright © Labour Friends of Israel 2005

The moral right of the authors has been asserted.

All rights reserved. Without limiting the rights under copyright reserved
above, no part of this publication may be reproduced, stored or
introduced into a retrieval system, or transmitted, in any form or by any
means (electronic, mechanical, photocopying, recording or otherwise),
without the prior written permission of both the copyright owner and
the publisher of this book.

A CIP catalogue record for this book is available from the British
Library.

ISBN 0 9500536 6 x

Typeset in Minion by MacGuru Ltd
info@macguru.org.uk

Printed and bound in Great Britain by Alden Group, Oxford

The views of the individual authors are not necessarily those of Labour
Friends of Israel.

Contents

Acknowledgements

This book was inspired by the many individuals who gave up their time and afforded the benefit of their wisdom, expertise and hospitality to the Labour Friends of Israel delegation of January 2005.

We are especially grateful to staff of the Ministry of Foreign Affairs for the activities and meetings in Israel; and to staff of the Palestinian Legislative Council for our enlightening and constructive experiences in and around Ramallah.

Thanks also go to the whole Labour Friends of Israel team, whose organisation, patience and industry delivered an itinerary reflecting the intricacies and emotions that have come to define this small but crucial part of the world.

LABOUR
LOOKS
AT
ISRAEL

27 CONTRIBUTORS

ERIC S. HEFFER, M.P.
PAUL ROSE, M.P.
RAYMOND FLETCHER, M.P.
TED ROWLANDS
DAVID MARQUAND, M.P.
RICHARD CROSSMAN, O.B.E., M.P.
Dr. EDWIN BROOKS
JOHN ELLIS
IAN MIKARDO, M.P.
GEOFFREY RHODES, M.P.
DENIS COE
LAURIE PAVITT, M.P.
CHRISTOPHER SEWELL

LESLIE HUCKFIELD, M.P.
ALAN FITCH, M.P.
Dr. MAURICE S. MILLER, M.P.
GOLDA MEIR
HARRY BAILEY
RODNEY BALCOMBE
ERNEST HAYHURST, O.B.E., J.P.
HERBERT KEMP, J.P.
ARTHUR W. J. LEWIS, M.P.
JAMES PATRICK ROCHE
MARGARET WATSON
TOM TORNEY, M.P.
TED LEADBITTER, M.P.

Price 30p.

Front cover of *Labour Looks at Israel*
(published by Labour Friends of Israel in 1971)

Editor's preface

The idea for this book occurred in the tranquil surroundings of the Sea of Galilee, with the mountains of the Golan Heights in the distance, and the mist rising from the calm water. Any visitor to Israel is struck by the incredible beauty of the country. For most, that awe is coupled with a sense of bewilderment and anger that such beautiful scenery can be scarred by such bitter conflict. Israel is a land of myths and contested histories – some stem from biblical times, some are as contemporary as yesterday. At the heart of the conflict are lies and propaganda, which serve only to promote distrust and fuel violence.

So nearly two dozen Labour politicians and activists went to Israel and the Palestinian Territories to see for ourselves, to ask difficult questions, to discuss politics with people of all persuasions, and to develop our own understanding. The Labour Friends of Israel (LFI) delegation in January 2005, led by Ivan Lewis MP, comprised Labour Members of Parliament, parliamentary candidates, MPs' researchers, Labour Party staff and a peer.

Labour politicians have been visiting Israel since the country gained independence in 1948, latterly more often than not under the aegis of Labour Friends of Israel. In 1971, a collection of essays by Labour visitors was published under the title *Labour Looks at Israel*, and that is where this collection gets its inspiration.

The essays collected here are personal views, selected to provide some illumination on each area under discussion. Each writer was asked to offer their own thoughts to help the reader understand a specific topic. The only stipulations were the word-count and the deadline, which the authors met with varying degrees of success. What follows is a series of pen-portraits of a land in a state of change and making painfully slow progress towards peace and security, written by some of the leading lights in the British Labour movement, in a spirit of solidarity and internationalism.

Events are moving so fast that already some of the impressions contained herein have been superseded by developments. Between the delegation returning to the UK and the time of publication, Tony Blair hosted a major summit on the Middle East, a bomb exploded in a nightclub a few yards from where the delegation was staying three weeks before, and Syria withdrew its troops from Lebanon. The essays should be viewed as snapshots, not definitive portraits.

If this book aids just a little in the process of peace, understanding and reconciliation, it will have been worthwhile.

Paul Richards
London, 2005

Foreword:
Labour looks to Israel

by Ivan Lewis MP

It was an honour for me to lead the largest ever Labour Friends of Israel delegation to Israel and the Palestinian Territories at one of the most dramatic and hopeful times in the recent history of the region.

The UK Labour Party has always taken a close interest in supporting the State of Israel, and there is a wide range of impassioned opinions about the region within our party. But the members of LFI know that the meaning of friendship is long-term commitment, in times of difficulty as well as celebration.

The enduring strength of LFI was made all the more clear to me by the uncovering in the LFI archives of a volume dating back to 1971. The booklet, entitled *Labour Looks at Israel,* is a compilation of nearly thirty essays from the Labour Party's leading lights of the day, writing about their experiences of visiting Israel following the 1967 Six Day War.

Familiar names in the list of contributors include David Marquand, Richard Crossman and Ian Mikardo. There is even a contribution from Israel's then Prime Minister, and one of the Jewish State's original socialist founders, Golda Meir.

That fascinating book is the inspiration for this new

compilation. Representatives of the LFI delegation from January 2005 followed in the footsteps of their predecessors and recorded their thoughts following their time spent in the region. Flicking through the pages of 1971's *Labour Looks at Israel*, one is struck by the remarkable similarity between the observations of delegates then and now.

David Marquand's contribution shows how immediately clear the dilemmas were to Israelis in the aftermath of the Six Day War. In words that are equally true today, Marquand writes:

> Every politically interested Israeli – and all Israelis seem to be politically interested – has his own plan for the peace settlement, for the refugees, for the West Bank. Many have more than one.

It is also remarkable to read his observation regarding the character of Israeli nationalism. Where he confesses he expected to find 'intransigent nationalism, tinged with chauvinism and perhaps militarism', in fact he observes 'The chauvinism and militarism are conspicuous by their absence.' Of the Israeli army, an institution that is central to the lives of all Israelis, because of the conscription of all the country's 18–21-year-olds, he makes a remark which I believe will still ring true for recent LFI visitors to Israel, saying:

> It is tough, well officered and well trained. But it is at the same time a civilian army, bent on returning as quickly as possible to its peacetime occupations, not on military conquest.

Richard Crossman, also preoccupied with the search for peace, makes further prescient observations. As well as remarkably stating that:

> I must admit that Israel is the only country apart from my own where I truly and deeply feel at home,

he notes that:

> I myself am convinced that it [peace] cannot emerge except by direct confrontation between the belligerents. No one else can make peace for the Jews and the Arabs.

Whilst we, as friends of Israel in the international community, continue to do all we can to support peace efforts, when spending time in the region one recognises immediately that no one could be more motivated and passionate about creating peace than the Israelis and Palestinians living with the pain of conflict.

The idea of this compilation is not only to convey a flavour of Israel's hopes and challenges from the perspective of UK representatives who have been there. The relationship between the UK and Israel, and the UK Labour Party and the Israeli Labor Party, as with all good relationships, should be two-way. It is not just Israel that stands to gain from its relationship with Britain, for we too have much we can learn from our Israeli friends and colleagues.

Whilst the 1971 booklet which inspired this volume was entitled *Labour Looks at Israel*, our 2005 version is entitled *Labour Looks to Israel*. We aim to assist, to encourage, sometimes to persuade, but also to learn.

A thread that runs through many of these contributions is that Israel's challenges are not far removed from our own. When Siôn Simon MP remarks on Israel's difficulties in balancing the need for national security with the strict demands of human rights, it brings to mind our own dilemmas in legislating to protect ourselves from terrorism.

When Linda Perham describes the revolutionary joint Jewish–Arab school in Israel, one thinks of our own challenges in developing a unified sense of national identity whilst preserving the rich cultural diversity we enjoy.

The importance of the broader regional context – both the challenges of regional reform, as discussed by Huw Irranca-Davies MP, and the strategic threats to Israel, as identified by Luke Akehurst – are immediately apparent when speaking to Israeli and Palestinian policy-makers. And the strategic issues will be familiar to followers of UK foreign policy priorities. Concerns are directed beyond the Palestinian Territories at Iran, the relationship between Lebanon and Syria, and the connections of each of these states to rejectionist groups in the peace process.

When I met officials in the Israeli education ministry, we were all struck by the similarities of the challenges we face, whether it is tackling truancy, raising standards or reforming the curriculum.

Some challenges, however, are unique to Israel's situation. Seeing Israel's armed forces at work, whether it be running an observation centre monitoring breaches of the security barrier, or eyeball to eyeball with Hezbollah outposts on the Lebanese border, one is struck firstly by their youth, and then by their sense of humour, camaraderie and duty. An impression of the remarkable and surprising encounters we had is the subject of Jennifer Gerber's essay.

Also unusual are the economic challenges caused by having to spend 7 per cent of GDP on defence at a time of economic contraction resulting from the impact of terrorism. Rachel Reeves turns an expert eye to economic issues, noting in particular the devastating impact of terror on the economy. She also considers the particular dilemmas created for the Israeli Labor Party in co-operating with the Likud, an arrangement which forces them to trade off economic policies to pursue the priority of disengagement.

One cannot speak about the challenges and hopes of Israel without considering the situation of their Palestinian neighbours. We spent time in the Palestinian Territories, meeting with Palestinian legislators and ministers at a time of dramatic, difficult, but exciting transition. The Palestinians are faced with the challenge of building a state, an issue on which Ashok Kumar MP reflects. On meeting Palestinian politicians, it appeared that, post-Arafat, it is a challenge they are confronting with a new-found sense of direction and determination.

The other issue covered in this volume is the relationship between the UK Labour Party and the Israeli Labor Party. In 1971, UK Labour MPs were still struck overwhelmingly by the extent to which Israel had been founded as a uniquely socialist democracy. Particular institutions such as the kibbutzim communal establishments and the powerful Histadrut Trade Union organisation deeply impressed them.

It is some years since the left wing dominated the Knesset as it did in the first decades of the state. But the Labor Party is fighting hard to maintain Israel's traditions as a society that cares for all its members, and as a country that seeks peace with its neighbours.

At the time of our visit, and at the time of writing, Labor has entered into a difficult partnership with the right-of-centre Likud. As one of the Labor Knesset Members told us, it is a partnership driven only by the overriding imperative to support the Prime Minister's steps to withdraw from Gaza and parts of the West Bank.

Many other dilemmas face the Israeli Labor Party, finding itself presented with the challenge of renewal after setbacks in the peace process and disappointments at the ballot box. These issues are considered by the editor of this book, Paul Richards.

But what seems beyond doubt when meeting Israeli Labor colleagues is that the ideals and hopes of Israel's leaders and parliamentarians are deeply linked to the views of many within our own party. With that thought in mind, I commend this collection of essays in the belief that in another thirty years, readers will be able to look back and know that the relationship between the UK Labour Party and the State of Israel was, in 2005, a bond of mutual respect, affection and strength.

UK and Israel: balancing security and human rights

by Siôn Simon MP

Upon appointment to the Home Office in 1965, Roy Jenkins said that the Department's purpose was 'that of striking a very difficult balance between the need to preserve the Queen's peace and the need to preserve the liberty of the individual'.

His time as Home Secretary is remembered for legislation on abortion, censorship and homosexuality that broadened individual liberties. Recently, with reference to ID cards or detention of terrorist suspects, Labour seems more likely to be charged with curtailing civil liberties. In the face of Al-Qaeda, the dilemma posed by Jenkins in 1965 is particularly acute today.

During the forty years since then, Britain responded to a heinous terrorist act in my city by detaining six innocent people under a draconian Terrorist Act, nodded through an obliging Parliament in one day, and allowing them to languish in jail for years. Few were the voices raised in protest during those years. Today, critics of Israel abound in the UK, but our response to the Birmingham pub bombing makes one wonder how Britain would have treated a security threat as intense as Israel's.

The IRA and Al-Qaeda are not the same. The IRA has a limited, specified aim; Al-Qaeda seeks to undermine the societies of the entire western world. Both threats are real and serious.

In Israel the immediacy of the terror threat is even more apparent. For example, bag searches are standard when entering a building. When B'Tselem, an Israeli human rights group, could report in November 2004 that more than 3,500 Palestinians and 927 Israelis died in the second Intifada, then such minor inconveniences pale. The UK does not have such a pervasive atmosphere of threat, but ID cards are, in an age when so much personal data is held by so many private and government agencies, a relatively minor concession to make in the fight against terrorism.

Widespread international condemnation would, however, suggest that the Israeli security fence involves the curtailment of too many rights in the name of security. Seeing a room filled with Israeli soldiers, many fulfilling their compulsory military service, staffing one of the fence's control centres – with all of the associated precision monitoring technology and weaponry – I was struck by the immense investment of financial and human resources required to maintain the barrier. At the same time I could not help but think of the inevitable intrusion on Palestinian movement and land caused by it.

While they monitor cameras patrolling the fence, 18-year-old Israeli soldiers text friends, perhaps making arrangements to meet in a night club – a suicide bomber's potential target. On the other side, Palestinians queue at despised check points, separated from land they have long farmed or water resources they have come to depend upon.

Yet on neither side can the benefits be discounted. The short-term benefits to Israel of preventing terror attacks could not be any more obvious. The number of successful attacks launched against Israeli civilians from the West Bank has fallen dramatically as a result of the fence. The barrier drastically increases the distance a potential suicide bomber has to travel, and Israeli security services have long understood that the further a bomber has to travel, the slimmer their chances of success.

But there is benefit also for the Palestinians, who have seen fewer armed Israeli incursions as a result. In the long term, both Israel and Palestine stand to gain from a reduction in the ill feeling that fuels terrorism, through this fall in armed Israeli incursions.

Indeed, 'Whoever doesn't work for the construction of a security fence,' claimed Eitan Cabel, a Labor Knesset member, in June 2003, 'will be responsible for the murder of Israeli citizens.' And Tony Blair recently argued with respect to the threat to the UK that:

> I think that this is terrorism without limit, and that in the use of suicide terrorists, it is different, so in those circumstances, for that limited number of cases, my best judgement is that considerations of national security have to come before civil liberties, no matter how important those civil liberties are.

Blair made this claim in response to criticism by Charles

Kennedy of the Terrorism Bill. The Bill itself was the government's response to the House of Lords ruling that aspects of the government's security policies breached human rights. Israeli law contains provision for the Israel Supreme Court, in a role comparable to the House of Lords in the UK, to be petitioned on any administrative decision of the state by any affected party, Israeli or Palestinian.

Much as the verdict of the House of the Lords has caused revision in the UK policy, the rulings of Israel's High Court of Justice have forced changes in Israeli government policy. The more than seventy petitions submitted to the Israeli Supreme Court since construction of the security fence began in 2002 have produced a number of significant changes in both the routing of the fence and the humanitarian arrangements to minimise disruption to local Palestinians. In both Israel and the UK, the executive has responded to judicial decisions by adapting policy, which has sparked lively debate on the balance between security measures and human rights.

Some contributions to these debates in both countries operate in theoretical terms, which fail to acknowledge the realities of life in these countries. Public debate about security in the UK is greatly skewed towards civil rights and against the right to be free from crime and disorder. In the beginning of 2005, the Lords gave their verdict on Belmarsh, and the Home Office published an independent review into the UK terrorist threat conducted by Lord Carlile. Both ought to be respected, but the prominence given to the former dwarfed that given to the latter, contributing to a public debate perversely out of kilter with the reality of the threat facing the UK.

This lends itself to mistrust of the state, which, given our genuine vulnerability to terrorism, is a dangerous development. For example, the state is treated with incredulity and dismissed by sections of the media when outlining the virtues of ID cards. At the same time the personal details stored by unaccountable private corporations, through supermarket discount cards, text messaging, bank accounts and other means, goes without comment.

Just as public debate in the UK on the correct balance between security measures and human rights ought to be reconfigured around the reality of the situation we live in, rather than around an abstract theoretical space, so too should our discussions about Israel.

The security fence, for example, is a complex issue, which should be understood in this way. Being even-handed requires us to think about lived realities on both sides of the conflict. Given that the route of the fence takes in major Jewish settlements, which have doubled in size since the signing of the Oslo accords a decade ago, Palestinian suspicions that the fence is a tool of Israeli territory-grab are understandable. But equally, with over 150,000 Israeli settlers living on just 5 per cent of the land along the Green Line, the demographic realities cannot be ignored.

In light of the demonstrations I witnessed outside the Knesset in opposition to the disengagement of around 8,000 Israelis from Gaza and the Northern West Bank, I recognise the political difficulties for Israel in evacuating even a small number of settlers. However, Palestinian desires for a future capital in east Jerusalem make settlements in this area a particularly difficult issue.

To be seen as a response to terrorism, and not a land-grab, the fence has to strike the optimum balance of protecting Israeli civilians whilst showing sensitivity to the interests of the Palestinians. The fence can help ensure that future negotiations are not destabilised by terrorism. But if the route of the fence is excessively invasive, its potential short-term stabilising effect would be negated by the deeper Palestinian antipathy it would invoke.

Though it is theoretically appealing to insist that the fence be entirely on Israeli territory, or exactly follow the 1967 borders, it is a pointless measure if it does not engage with the reality of the security threat. For example, one of the fence's detours has prevented successful rocket attacks on civilian aircraft taking off from Ben Gurion Airport. The most sensible way forward with regard to the route is to look sensitively at the realities of life on both sides. It is heartening that the Israeli cabinet announced in late February changes to the route of the fence that brings it much closer to the Green Line than before. The amount of territory captured by Israel in 1967 remaining on the Israeli side of the fence will fall to 8 per cent, half of the land mass contained in the 2003 barrier proposal.

The Israeli Government insists that the fence is not a border. Hopefully the barrier, along its new route, will help both sides come closer to a situation where a permanent border, acceptable to all, can be mutually agreed.

Internal Israeli debate on the fence has been vigorous; as has the check placed on the Israeli executive by the judiciary. Israel wants to remain Jewish and democratic. A broad consensus in Israel understands this necessitates territorial compromise with the Palestinians. Palestine wants to become democratic and autonomous, following the path of compromise with Israel, rather than conflict. These were certainly the trends I detected during my time in the region. But the long walk to statehood and stability is notoriously littered with agonising pitfalls in this part of the world.

In light of September 11, the UK has been forced to readdress the balance between security and civil liberties to take account of a terror threat similar to that which has long hung over Israel. But for Israel the challenge has more fundamental implications for creating a future of peace and co-existence. This end point requires Israel to reconcile itself once and for all, as it has at every major junction since the 1937 Peel Commission report, to demographics over geography. Population projections are such that Israel cannot be democratic and Jewish without permanently relinquishing territories it has controlled since 1967. The Palestinians for their part have to completely accept and accommodate the existence of Israel.

An acceptance of shared rights marks the end of the journey but, as I have tried to illustrate, we will travel more lightly if we focus less on the theoretical underpinnings of these rights and more on applying them to the world as it is.

The economy, prosperity and peace

by Rachel Reeves

Israel is one of the most high-tech nations, economcentres
the world. Information and communication technologies,
research and development are big business. The economy
is more hi-tech than the US, and Israel comes third

The economy, prosperity and peace

by Rachel Reeves

The poor, the vulnerable and the weakest in society pay the highest cost for war and insecurity. Peace is a pre-condition for sustainable economic growth and prosperity, and for reducing inequality. Economic integration and regeneration can also help drive forward the peace process. The Israeli Labor Party needs a positive and visionary economic agenda – to push for economic policies to help Israel now, and on its path towards peace.

Inequality and conflict

Since the establishment of the State of Israel in 1948, the levels of sustained growth, despite the challenges of absorbing huge numbers of immigrants and facing a constant security threat, have been described at times as an 'economic miracle'. Even today, after a difficult period during the Intifada, Israel's economy places it in the top 30 countries in the world for per capita income.

Israel is one of the most high-tech intensive economies in the world. Information and communication technologies, research and development are big business. The economy is more ICT intensive than the US, and Israel comes third for the number of companies listed on the high-tech New York stock exchange, Nasdaq, after the US and Canada. These are facts that were perhaps a little surprising to me as a first-time visitor to Israel, but the young, highly educated and ambitious workforce have created in the Middle East a vibrant and dynamic economy.

However, for insecurity, war and instability, you pay a heavy price. For the poor, the vulnerable and weak that price is higher still. It is a price paid directly and indiscriminately – with killings, destruction of property and the corrosive element of fear. But there are also indirect costs. Businesses close, investment declines and government spending shifts to defence and security.

During the second Intifada tourism fell by 50 per cent. Restaurants, bars, clubs and hotels closed down. The hardest hit have been the lowest skilled – the waiters, cleaners and construction workers.

And insecurity and violence skews government spending. Israel has to spend about 7 per cent of GDP on defence, compared with 2.5 per cent in the UK.

In a country historically rich in social solidarity, the past decade has seen a fall in government spending per capita on health and education of about 20 per cent. Israel's Thatcherite Likud Finance Minister, Benjamin Netanyahu, has limited growth in government spending, excluding defence, to 1 per cent a year.

Inequality is on the rise in Israel. Yora Gabay, chairman of Peilim Portfolio Management and former Director of State Revenue at the Ministry of Finance, argues that government policy is a big factor behind the increase. While the wealthy raise their spending to make up for the cuts in government provision, the poor, who are the biggest consumers of government spending, see falls in the services they receive.

Unemployment in Israel has fallen in the last year and hovers at around 10 per cent. This is comparable to Germany and France, and about twice as high as in the UK and US. Economic inactivity – those neither in work, nor seeking work, is about twice as high as in western Europe (in part reflecting choices in some very orthodox Jewish communities about the balance between work and religious activity). Even many of those who do work often live in poverty. Zvi Zussman, former deputy governor of the Bank of Israel, reports that 'half of Israel's poor have jobs. Their poverty is not due to working or old age, but to low wages for their work.'

Tough competition in the labour market has forced many Israelis to take jobs paying less than the official minimum wage. The average hourly wage rate in Israel has fallen by 7 per cent in the last year.

In Palestine, the economic condition is much worse, and as in Israel, it is made worse still by conflict. Since the outbreak of the Intifada in 2000, the Palestinian economy has lost an estimated $4.5 billion, a 30 per cent fall in per capita GDP. Unemployment stands at about 25–30 per cent and has risen sharply through the course of the Intifada. Output is extremely volatile, in large part because of the frequent closures and special security measures taken by Israel. When we visited Ramallah in January 2005, both unemployment and underemployment were highly evident.

In the past, many Palestinians have worked in Israel,

where wages are higher and jobs relatively more available. Ninety per cent of the value of imports and 70 per cent of the value of exports come from Israel. So Palestinians are hugely dependent on Israel for jobs and growth. Conflict, closed borders and mistrust have a direct impact on the economic well-being of Palestinians.

Peace, stability and growth

The high-tech boom and bust is part of the reason for Israel's woes since 2000. But Shlomo Swirski of the Adva Centre, a Tel Aviv-based social policy think tank, says that the cost of the Intifada over four and a half years is $30–40 billion, about ten times higher than the cost of the high-tech bust in 2000/2001. Even the most conservative estimates put the cost at around $12 billion. Swirski argues that the only lasting solution to Israel's economic malaise is a political solution to the Palestinian–Israeli conflict, including Israeli withdrawal from Gaza and the West Bank.

The economic cost of the Intifada demands a political response. The response from Israel must be two-fold. First, in order for Israel to continue to be an attractive country for continued Jewish immigration, and to continue to be a country with a bright economic future, efforts to find a sustainable, peaceful co-existence with all her neighbours must be stepped up. Secondly, during the journey to a lasting and viable peace, the government has a duty to protect its citizens, both physically and economically, from the cruel burdens of the conflict.

For every year of the Intifada, Israeli GDP has been about 3–7 per cent lower than would have been the case without the conflict. An end to the conflict is the surest way out of economic hardship for thousands of Israelis.

Some on the Israeli right argue that peace is not a necessary condition for growth. This flies in the face of the facts. Without peace, insecurity will continue. At the same time the huge drain on resources eats away at economic growth and renewal.

Looking back at the history of Israel, there is a clear, positive correlation between economic growth and political stability. Israel's first Prime Minister, David Ben Gurion, reduced defence spending, and growth was high and robust. Between 1950 and 1965 growth was strong, despite intermittent violence and the Sinai campaign. Instability during this period was largely confined to the borders, thus having a less marked effect on overall economic conditions. From 1973 to 1985, defence spending rose to an average of 25 per cent of GDP and growth fell to zero. In the early 1990s, Prime Minister Yitzhak Rabin managed greatly to reduce the level of conflict and cut defence spending, and economic growth picked up.

Israel and Palestine can learn a lot from the experience in Europe – economic engagement can foster improved political relations, and peace can drive economic growth and regeneration. Cross-border trade works best when it is conducted in security and with stable trading partners. Israel and Palestine would benefit from increased stability, from freer movement of labour and capital, and from increased and less volatile trade with each other and with other neighbouring states.

This is increasingly the case in a globalised world economy, where money and capital move freely. Israel is a small, open economy. Trade, inward investment and tourism are integral ingredients for economic growth. Without secure borders and stable production chains, trade is difficult. Businesses crave stability, and investment needs long time horizons. Without security and stability there is a high risk premium on investment in infrastructure and technology – estimated at about an extra 30 per cent on the costs of production in 2004. And without security, tourism will not pick up to support the fledgling economic recovery.

As well as being part of the prize of a peace settlement, economic integration and co-operation could form part of the solution. It is in the interest of Israel and Palestine to become more interdependent economically, in order to reduce the incentives to prolong the conflict. If your liveli-hood is linked to that of your neighbour, it becomes increas-ingly crazy to engage in violence. Economic interdependence will not break the deadlock. But it can be another means of chipping away at the barriers to peace.

An economic agenda for Labor
Peace requires a political settlement, and continued conflict signifies political failure. If politicians cannot find a political solution, then they have a responsibility to do everything in their power to protect society from the consequences of the continued impasse. This means facilitating economic security as well as physical security.

Under Prime Minister Rabin, with the defence budget falling, Israel was able to invest in public services and assist immigrant absorption through transfer payments. Under Sharon and Netanyahu, transfer payments have been cut back sharply.

Of course, there are strong economic arguments for welfare-to-work policies – both Democrats in the US and the UK Labour Party have made the economic and social inclusion arguments for such policies. But welfare-to-work policies and linking social security payments to taking a job or training rely on an economy with jobs available to take. In Israel, jobs are scarce. Cutting transfer payments will only make the poor worse off. The government has not helped by cutting the wages of public sector workers and freezing public infrastructure projects – especially as construction is one of the industries hardest hit by the Intifada.

Although Keynesian economics has not been fashionable since the late 1970s, when there is a clear problem of insufficient demand, the government can play an important role in kick-starting the economic recovery.

Israeli Labor and those on the left are in a predicament. To ensure that disengagement in Gaza and parts of the West Bank occur, Labor must continue to be a prop for Likud. But support comes at a heavy price for many Labor Members of the Knesset.

Collette Avital and Yuli Tamir, two Labor Members of the Knesset (MKs), put this in sharp focus while we were in Israel. They talked of battles with their conscience in supporting Likud's free market and laissez-faire policies. While Netanyahu talks of dismantling the welfare state, Labor MKs believe it is more crucial than ever. With new immigrants to be absorbed, often from Africa, with little in the way of skills or savings, and with the number living in poverty – both in and out of work – higher than ever, surely the welfare state has a critical role. Israel's history of being a country rich in social solidarity is under attack from the policies of Likud.

Israel's Labor Party must argue more vociferously for a new economic strategy that will lift Israel from the recent history of stagnation and sharp increases in inequality.

In this respect Israeli Labor can learn from its sister parties, especially in the UK and US. A positive agenda needs to be outward-looking. Israel's high-tech 'miracle', with sharp rises in productivity and high rates of business start-ups, needs to be nurtured and built upon.

Training in lifelong learning and school education should be geared towards ensuring that all Israelis, whether first, second or third generation, have the skills to enable them to compete in the new economy. And to bring back inward investors, the peace process needs to be resumed. Tax credits to encourage investment, especially in key sectors like R&D and ICT, could be introduced to help compensate for the security premium on investment. Such policy challenges are not a hundred miles away from those faced in the UK in the first decade of the 21st century. However, while these are key and focal issues in the UK, in Israel they often fall by the wayside because debate and political priorities are dominated by defence and security.

Like everything else in Israel, a lasting solution to economic problems has to take into account security concerns. The political case for economic co-operation with Palestine, as well as the moral one, needs to be made more strongly. Increasing the number of work permits available to Palestinians, allowing a greater volume of imports, including imports with higher value added, would foster goodwill and increase interdependency. Israel needs also to make sure that the security fence fulfils its purpose and cuts the number of suicide bombings, but that it doesn't further alienate and impoverish Palestinians, who risk being cut off from their work or land. The international community too has a role, to help rebuild the Palestinian infrastructure and productive capacity, to enable Palestine to be a viable economic partner with Israel.

But all this should be backed up by what Israel and Israeli Labor stand for: social solidarity and support. The Jewish homeland must protect, nurture and support all its citizens – Jewish and non Jewish. A precondition for this in the long term is peace, stability and co-operation with the emerging Palestinian state.

Roadblocks on the Roadmap: Iran, Syria, Lebanon and Hezbollah

by Luke Akehurst

Before visiting Israel in January this year and meeting senior officials involved with Israel's strategic planning, I had assumed, like most British political observers, that Israel's main security threat was terrorism in the form of 'suicide bombings' by extremist Palestinian factions. My visit to Israel highlighted the fact that there are myriad other security threats that face the country over the months and years to come.

It seems clear to me that there is commonality between Israeli and UK security interests, since Israel's main threats in the region are forces that oppose democratic development and the Roadmap as two sides of the same coin. Israel's principal enemy is by no means the Palestinian people. On the contrary, moderate Israelis and Palestinians, and those in the international community who support the Roadmap, share a common enemy: those forces that oppose the peace process and broader regional reform for their own strategic political and geopolitical reasons. Standing on the Israeli–Lebanese border and looking across at a Hezbollah lookout post a few hundred metres away, the immediacy of the regional threat to Israel and the peace process is all the more apparent.

Iranian nuclear programme

The most potent and immediate potential threat to Israel is that Iran may develop nuclear weapons.

Israel's alarm that Iran may reach a 'point of no return' in nuclear technology has been growing over recent years. The E3 (Germany, France and the UK) have been in a long series of talks on a suspension agreement with Tehran over its nuclear programme, during which Iran continues to seek major economic and technological concessions. What seems clear is that the E3 have had difficulty persuading Iran that developing nuclear weapons is not in its own interest. Iran's imminent acquisition of nuclear weapons could undermine Middle East stability in various ways:

- Iran already sponsors radical groups in the region, such as Hezbollah, to further their geopolitical interests. An Iran with a nuclear deterrent could behave more aggressively towards other countries in order to advance its regional interests and influence.
- A nuclear Iran could become the cornerstone of Islamic radicalism in the Middle East, and the dominant military power in the region, strengthening radical regimes and movements.
- The acquisition of nuclear weapons by Iran would pressure other regional powers, such as Egypt, Syria or Saudi Arabia, to join the nuclear club, thus triggering a regional nuclear arms race.

- Iran has developed Shihab 3 medium-range ballistic missiles with a range of 1,300 km, and its Shihab 4 is expected to reach 2,000 km. They could carry chemical or nuclear warheads to EU and NATO states as well as Israel.
- The damage done by Iranian acquisition of nuclear warheads to the UK's attempts at promoting the Roadmap and regional development and to Israel's immediate security cannot be underestimated.

Syrian support for terrorism

Of Israel's immediate neighbours, Syria remains the Arab state least open to peaceful coexistence. It retains large armed forces, modelled for offensive warfare. However, these are armed and organised on outdated Soviet lines and are not considered a match for the Israel Defence Forces (IDF), which has embraced the modern technologies and doctrines associated with Network Centric Warfare.

The real threat to Israel's security currently presented by Syria is that it shelters and provides a base for terrorist organisations. Hezbollah, Hamas and the Popular Front for the Liberation of Palestine (PFLP) all have offices in Damascus. Khaled Mashal, Chairman of the Hamas Political Office and de facto leader of the organisation, resides in Syria under the protection of the Syrian government.

These groups all promote continued armed struggle rather than a peace process, and are as much enemies of the moderate Palestinian leadership as they are of Israel. The Palestinian ministers who met with our delegation in Ramallah acknowledged that there is little commonality of interest between Iran and Syria and the Palestinian leadership. The two regional powers have a geopolitical interest in continuing conflict rather than a peaceful solution in Gaza and the West Bank.

The bomb attack on a Tel Aviv nightclub on Friday 25 February 2005 was clearly designed to try to derail the peace process. Israel sees Syria as the likely culprit, and Palestinian leader Mahmoud Abbas described it as an 'act of sabotage' by a 'third party'.

Israel's Foreign Minister Silvan Shalom said:

> We see Syria as responsible by allowing those extremists to have their headquarters there, their training camps there and to give them all the assistance that they're asking.

A recent Russia–Syria missile deal included short-range anti-aircraft missiles. The deal was condemned by the US, EU, and Israel, as they fear that the weapons may be obtained by terrorists, particularly Hezbollah, and used against civilian airliners or coalition troops in Iraq. It also seemed to contradict Russia's involvement in the Roadmap as a member of the Quartet.

The growing influence of Hezbollah

Our delegation stood on the Israeli–Lebanese border and observed the eyeball-to-eyeball strategic face-off between Israel and the Syrian and Iranian-backed Hezbollah. Hezbollah is effectively a proxy militia army for its Syrian and Iranian paymasters, and it is so well armed and militarily proficient that even the IDF is warily respectful.

Although the IDF withdrew from Lebanon in May 2000, and the UN Security Council declared that the withdrawal complied with Resolution 425, Hezbollah continues attacking Israel along its border with Lebanon and in the Har Dov (Shebaa Farms) region, which is part of the Golan Heights. Since May 2000, Hezbollah has attacked the IDF at Har Dov 33 times, killing ten and wounding dozens.

In a new development in 2004, Hezbollah extended its activities in Israel by planning and directing terrorist cells operating inside the West Bank and Gaza. Last year, Israel's domestic security agency identified 51 Hezbollah-operated Palestinian groups, 38 of which were Fatah affiliated. Israeli officials stress that Hezbollah pay well, in cash, for suicide and terror attacks, a role increasingly acknowledged by Palestinians in discussion with the delegation.

Iran–Syria alliance
The announcement in February of an Iran–Syria security alliance further emphasised the threat to regional security posed by two of the foremost supporters of terrorism.

Their co-operation is a marriage of convenience between two ideologically disparate regimes – the Islamist theocracy in Iran and the secular Arab nationalism of Syria – to head off what they perceive as a common threat from the West.

The role of incitement
Incitement to anti-Israeli violence in the Iranian, Syrian and Lebanese media is the continuation of the conflict through propaganda means. Television stations such as Lebanon's

Hezbollah channel, al-Manar, and Iranian state satellite channel Sahar TV broadcast overtly antisemitic and extreme anti-Israel programmes that seek to spread hatred of Jews and Israel around the world, undermining efforts to promote the peace process. Education systems in Arab states dismiss the legitimacy of the State of Israel and demonise Jews and Judaism. These factors help explain the continued ability of terrorist groups to find willing young recruits. There is an alarming parallel between the modern role of satellite TV channels in promoting anti-Israeli violence and the similar role played by radio stations such as Cairo's Voice of the Arabs in the build-up to the Six Day War in 1967.

Conclusion

The UK in particular and the West in general need to understand that the conflict in the Middle East is not just a bi-polar one between Israel and the Palestinians. There are other regional powers that have their own religious or political agendas that cause them to undermine the peace process, and with it the future prosperity and autonomy of the Palestinian people, of whom they present themselves as allies. Constantly upping the ante of the 'struggle against Zionism' in Damascus and Tehran helps channel domestic anger against an external target rather than the repressive regime at home. It provides the population in many Arab countries with a scapegoat to blame for the poverty, under-development, corruption and political repression that have in fact been largely caused by their own regimes.

In its mildest form, this continued hostility to Israel helps act as a media and educational recruiting sergeant for terrorism. In its intermediate stage it involves the actual funding and arming of terrorist groups by third-party countries who want to keep the conflict going. In its most extreme form, it involves Iran trying to acquire weapons of mass destruction so that it can marry its avowed intention to destroy Israel with the actual military capability to do so.

The era in which Israel had to fight pitched tank battles with its Arab neighbours for survival in 1967 and 1973 has now passed, in part because of the realisation by Israel's neighbours that these were battles they could not win.

However, at least two states, Iran and Syria, remain firmly opposed to the peace process and have now started to employ proxy terrorists, and in Iran's case also to develop WMDs, to enable them to sustain their conflict with the State of Israel.

The great tragedy is that just as the Palestinians were the main victims of the misguided attempt by the Arab states to destroy Israel in 1967, leading to the occupation by Israel of Gaza and the West Bank, so the Palestinian people are the main victims of a situation where Iran and Syria are sabotaging the infant peace process. A cynic might think that there are forces in the wider Middle East who don't want to see a democratic, secular Palestinian state co-existing peacefully with Israel, for the signals that would send and the model it would give to their own peoples.

Palestine: building a democratic neighbourhood

by Ashok Kumar MP

The Labour Friends of Israel delegation to Israel and Palestine was my second opportunity to visit the area in five years and it filled me with a new sense of hope and optimism. Visiting Ramallah highlighted, for me, the enormous potential for development and reform as well as the momentous challenges which face Israelis, Palestinians and the international community as a whole.

Following Israel's planned withdrawal from the Gaza Strip in 2005, and under a new democratically elected leader, the Palestinian Authority now has the challenge – and the opportunity – to build a stable, democratic state alongside Israel.

Repeated statements from both Israel and the international community have emphasised that only an open and democratic Palestinian State will satisfactorily resolve the conflict. It was clear to our delegation, in speaking to both Israelis and Palestinians, that Palestinian President Mahmoud Abbas and his new leadership must undertake a wide-ranging programme of political, security and economic reforms to establish the basis for overcoming the chaos that has characterised the Palestinian Territories in the past few years.

Political reform

One of the key objectives for the UK, US, EU and G8 is to initiate democratic reform in the Middle East that will allow the further development of peace and security in the region. The election of Mahmoud Abbas as Palestinian President provides an opportunity for Palestinians to be liberated from the autocratic and corrupt structures of an apparatus that had become an end in itself.

Abbas firmly believes that the era of suicide bombing did great harm to the Palestinian cause. He is determined to advance that cause with negotiations and to encourage Palestinian militants to put down their weapons. His policy throughout the leadership election was to return to the Roadmap, end the violence and move towards negotiation. The fact that this approach has been overwhelmingly supported by the Palestinian people has, I believe, given him a fresh and democratic mandate with which to carry through his proposed reforms.

On our visit to the territories, just two weeks after the Palestinian Presidential elections on 9 January 2005, it was apparent that the elections were filled with the promise of a better future and could spell a new and brighter era of progress for Palestinian politics and the politics of the region as a whole. Yet, in order to reverse the autocratic and dictatorial style of the previous government and create a fully democratic state, there must be continued progress and a determined push towards establishing the key features that characterise a genuine democracy. These include freedom of speech and expression, a free press, a commitment to upholding human rights, adherence to the rule of law, reform of the judiciary and, most significantly in this case, the ability to monopolise the use of force under a unified and accountable Palestinian National Authority.

Democratisation on this scale is no easy or short-term feat, but it is essential that Abbas and his leadership are fully committed to the establishment of these democratic features. Hope can be drawn from the vigilance of Palestinian Legislative Council (PLC) members who forced Ahmed Qurei, the Palestinian Prime Minister, to scrap his initial proposed cabinet list over fears it was stacked with members of the old guard. A new cabinet of reformers can now pave the way for Mahmoud Abbas to press ahead with a promised overhaul of the Palestinian Authority. With the majority of Palestinian legislators determined to break from the past, there are signs of a genuine Palestinian commitment to negotiation and reform.

On the very same day that the delegation was in Ramallah, we were told by the PLC representives we met that President Abbas was attempting to negotiate with militants. There is a temporary lull in violence and it seems that many of the militants associated with Hamas, Islamic Jihad and the Al Aqsa Martyrs Brigade have, for the time being, put down their weapons. But it remains to be seen whether a permanent ceasefire will follow, laying the foundations for political negotiation to replace military action in furthering their goals. When Sharon and Abbas met in February 2005 there were positive signs of a more peaceful future. Yet, as with the Camp David Accords in 1978 and the Oslo Accords, signs of promise must be met with the keeping of promises. If the peaceful situation develops then maybe the Intifada could be considered to be over. Only then will we know whether the increasing politicisation of Hamas will result in a more moderate organisation that embraces a two-state solution, or whether it will serve simply as political cover for its military movement.

In order to smooth the process of peace it will, I believe, be necessary for the Palestinian Authority – whilst protecting press freedom – to prevent extreme antisemitic and anti-Israel incitement in the Palestinian media and in their education system. The new Palestinian leadership must limit the flow of propaganda that generates violence and inevitably undermines any attempts to establish peace. In this area, Abbas has made some progress, but to reduce incitement and deep-rooted animosity the reforms must be focused throughout all layers of Palestinian society. Although this is a long-term issue, requiring a long-term solution, it is necessary for the Palestinian Authority to assess the school curriculum and revise offending and provocative aspects. This will be a real test for Abbas and his leadership and an opportunity for him to create a freer and more liberated Palestine.

Security reform

Reform of the Palestinian security services is an integral part of the process of building a democratic neighbour to Israel, which is necessary to the success of the peace process. Conflict and animosity have been deepened by constant and damaging external, violent influences, and these must be tackled. During the visit the challenge of dealing with these violent influences was raised with Palestinian interlocutors. They acknowledged the damage caused by Syria and Iran in financially backing extremists and terrorist groups. This is a significant problem for the Palestinians, which they struggle to deal with. They stressed that Palestinian security forces are limited in their resources and President Abbas must even ask permission to fly to Gaza from the West Bank. In addition they made clear that the Palestinian Authority has never had any influence over Iran or Syria.

The situation for the Palestinian people is such that it has always been difficult to make the case that the moderate approach is the best way forward. Another destructive external influence is that of Hezbollah, something that was stressed to us by the Israeli foreign ministry analysts we met during our visit. Israel's security services have highlighted the increasing influence of Hezbollah on Palestinian terror groups. A key problem is that they reward Palestinian groups in cash for carrying out terror attacks. For the Palestinian Authority to exert lasting control over their territories, address this Hezbollah infiltration, and establish a degree of stability, full international cooperation is necessary.

Economic reform

As a result of the second Intifada, since September 2000 the Palestinian economy has lost an estimated $4.5 billion and unemployment has risen as high as 31 per cent. The living standards of ordinary Palestinian men and women are unsatisfactory, with over 60 per cent living below the poverty line. The delegation of Palestinians we met during our visit expressed the hardships they have experienced in recent years. Thus, the Palestinian economy relies heavily on funding from international donors, including £40 million from the UK Department for International Development in 2003.

The two principal benefits of disengagement for the Palestinian economy are as follows. Firstly, Israeli withdrawal from the Gaza Strip brings down at least some of the barriers to internal mobility which have existed over the past few years. It opens the main north–south, Erez–Rafah road and allows access for Palestinians to areas that are currently prohibited. Although this may bring immediate relief, for any significant long-term economic benefit there needs to be a wholesale redevelopment of the transport infrastructure. This would improve the flow of goods to people, significantly improving their situation. Secondly, with the settlements currently held by Israel handed over to the Palestinians, around 70 square kilometres of fertile agricultural land provides an added resource for the Gaza economy. However, this land is only useful if there are markets for the produce and a means of transporting goods out of Gaza.

Israel's disengagement plan has direct implications for the state of the Palestinian economy and for the future economic relations between the two peoples. Security is a prerequisite to investment and economic regeneration. Increased security will raise the confidence of donors and will encourage investors. The measure and scope of the reforms that will take place in the Palestinian Territories remain to be seen, but there is considerable international will to assist the process, something which presents a real opportunity for peace and reconciliation between Israelis and Palestinians.

Labour looks to Israel – the UK engagement

Our government, and especially Tony Blair himself, has put the UK at the heart of the pursuit of peace in the Middle East. The Prime Minister and Foreign Secretary are convinced that a solution to the Israeli–Palestinian conflict is an important precondition for long-term security. Peace in the region will inevitably benefit the international community as a whole. The UK government has helped pave the way towards a renewed peace process through steadfast support for the Quartet backed Roadmap to peace. In addition, the UK government has supported the Palestinians in developing their security apparatus by setting up two operation rooms, one in Gaza and one in Ramallah, and the establishment of civil police support that is now being supported by the EU. A financial investigation unit has been set up by the UK to scrutinise money transfers and tackle foreign influence on the ground. Possibly the most influential UK involvement, however, was the initiation of the London conference which took place on 1 March 2005. This initiative began the process of marshalling international support and setting the parameters and expectations for reform as Palestine moves to establishing a democratic and stable state.

The involvement and support of the international community as a whole is essential to continuation of negotiations and the establishment of peace in the Middle East. Significant progress has been made, with the recent release of Palestinian prisoners (the largest in a decade) and the decision by the Israeli cabinet to remove settlers from the Gaza Strip and parts of the West Bank. But, of course, there is still a lot to be done, and the Palestinian Authority must rise to the challenge that faces it, to build a stable, democratic state to exist alongside Israel, and put an end to the violence that has plagued the region. In order to achieve this, the international community must fulfil its own responsibility and continue to push for peace. In looking to the Middle East, Britain and the region itself can look with optimism for the future.

Arab and Jewish grassroots dialogue: challenging perceptions

by Linda Perham

Some people think that Arabs and Jews hate each other, and always will. End of story. Obviously, atrocities have happened in Israel and the media has a duty to report these. However, at times it seems that this duty does not stretch to reporting the successful efforts made by both sides to improve understanding and relations between the two communities. There is more to Arab–Jewish relations than suicide bombings, terrorist attacks, imposed curfews and military activity.

As a Member of Parliament between 1997 and 2005, I was privileged through my dealings with Labour Friends of Israel to have been on three delegations to Israel. My former constituency of Ilford North has about 9,000 Jewish residents, and I always enjoyed close links with them.

On my latest trip to Israel earlier this year, I visited a Hand-in-Hand school in Kfar Kara in the Wadi Ara region. Wadi Ara is a predominantly Arab region, although there are Jewish inhabitants too. Like most others with an interest in the topic, I recognise that the Arab–Israeli conflict is very delicate and there is no clear and easy solution. However, all efforts undertaken to improve relations between Arab and Jewish children can only lead to a better and brighter future.

There are three Hand-in-Hand centres for Jewish–Arab education: one in the Galilee, one in Jerusalem, and the one I visited in Kfar Kara. The first centres were established in 1997, and the school in Wadi Ara was opened in September 2004. Each school has two principals, one Jewish and one Arab. In addition, each classroom has one Arab and one Jewish teacher and the students are encouraged to speak both Arabic and Hebrew. Lessons are conducted in both languages.

The schools were initiated at a time when few could contemplate mixing Arab and Jewish children in the Israeli education system, but today these schools have the full recognition and backing of the Israeli Ministry of Education. The primary principle of these schools is to teach pupils about Muslim, Christian and Jewish cultures and holidays. Through the twin towers of understanding and respect, relations are improving. These are very exciting and encouraging times indeed!

Societies around the world have had to deal with the difficulties of integrating ethnic groups. It is heartening to see those challenges being tackled in Israel. About 20 per cent of the population is Arab and the schooling system has traditionally been segregated, with two separate curricula for Arab and Jewish students. I hope these Hand-in-Hand centres represent a watershed in the relationship between Israel's Arab and Jewish citizens.

Realism also plays a part in this initiative. The concept

of mixed schools brings up certain issues, and plain sailing it certainly is not. One such problem, I learned, centred on Israel's Independence Day. The Jewish population see the occasion as a national holiday and a reason for rejoicing. However, for Arabs, the day has very different connotations. Issues such as this are not side-stepped but are discussed, with ample opportunity for the pupils to voice their opinions. Another recent example was the death of Yasser Arafat. Arab children had grown up with the image of Arafat as a figure-head, whilst for many Jews he was seen as an enemy. But despite the differences of views, his death was not ignored. In fact, time was set aside for the pupils to share their divergent perspectives.

To have ideals is one thing, but to actively promote these, and tackle demanding situations head-on, is the only way that significant improvements will be made. The dedica-tion of the founders and teachers at these centres should be admired. I feel that their perseverance and dedication will find its legacy in the opinions of the pupils they are in contact with daily.

I have always believed that racism, intolerance and hatred between different religious communities is unnatural. People will generally get on with other people and it is only prejudice on both sides that stops this. A pilot programme was recently introduced in fourteen elementary schools in northern Israel whereby conversational Arabic is taught to fifth-grade students – alongside studies of Arabic culture and traditions. This widens the understanding of opposing views and also makes it easier for Jews and Arabs to commu-nicate.

All members of Labour Friends of Israel want to see a peaceful solution to Arab–Jewish tensions and, as we all know, this will take time to achieve. However, I am of the opinion that these Hand-in-Hand centres will go a long way in helping forge a common identity. Hand-in-Hand also hopes to open more schools, kindergartens and primary and secondary schools. Increasing mutual trust, understanding and appreciation of other cultures does not detract from one's own identity.

I would also like to mention Givat Haviva, the Jewish–Arab Centre for Peace, which I, along with other MPs, also visited on the LFI delegation. Founded in 1949, Givat Haviva is the national education centre of the Kibbutz Artzi Movement, a federation of 83 kibbutzim throughout the nation. It conducts seminars and workshops, hosts conferences, and offers formal and informal educational programmes for adults and children in a broad range of fields.

The movement still promotes the principles upon which Israel was founded. It acknowledges the reality that Israel is a multi-cultural democratic state and that equal rights for all citizens are an essential component. Givat Haviva also believes that education is the most important contribution that can be made for future generations and seeks to challenge existing stereotypes.

As an elected representative, I was so proud to do what I could to encourage, promote and foster these developments. I know the Jewish community in Ilford North aspire as I do to a time when there will be a peaceful state of Israel. However, I do not believe this can be accomplished without full input from both sides.

Education is not the only path, and I would also highlight what sport has done to engender co-existence. Bnei Sakhnin FC became the first Arab-owned football club to win the Israeli Cup, and went on to play Newcastle United in the UEFA Cup. The club has an Arab chairman, a Jewish coach and a mix of Christian, Jewish and Muslim playing staff. The Israeli national team has also been at the forefront of bridging the gap and has capped several Arab players in recent years. Recently, Walid Badir, formerly of Wimbledon FC, was the first Israeli Arab to wear the captain's armband. I find this particularly uplifting: Muslims, Jews and Christians playing together with one intention – an Israeli victory. To quote Willy Brandt's immortal words, 'What belongs together is growing together.'

Long may it continue.

Israeli army and Israeli society: meeting Israel's teenage soldiers

by Jennifer Gerber

Israeli soldiers seem to conjure up many different images for many different people. From symbol of statehood, to illegal occupier, the IDF (Israel Defence Forces) evoke a range of emotions.

On our trip to Israel, the Labour Friends of Israel delegation had a chance to meet for themselves members of the IDF. For many, this was their first experience of coming face to face with an Israeli soldier. Any preconceptions people had were soon to be challenged.

Certainly in the British media, Israel's soldiers generally do not get a good press. Of course, there have been incidents involving the IDF that have warranted international scrutiny, but remarkably little has been written on the wider context in which Israel's armed forces operate.

To understand the attitudes and values of the Israeli army, it helps to look at a few basic facts. Often people are unaware that most of the army is made up of civilian conscripts and that in many cases women can play as full a role as men. Conscription extends to all Israelis as they reach the age of

18, and the period of service is three years for men and 21 months for women. Men then remain as reservists for up to 30 years, spending as much as one month a year on active duty.

As one might expect of a 'civilian' army, the IDF is responsive to the cultural and social needs of its soldiers, running educational programmes and personal support services. Recruits with incomplete educational backgrounds are often given opportunities to upgrade their level of learning. This is particularly important for a society that is constantly absorbing large numbers of immigrants from countries around the world, many of whom may still be grappling with the language. From the time of Israel's founding, its first Prime Minister, David Ben Gurion, saw the IDF as a melting pot in which to bind together Israel's diverse population.

Some units in the army are dedicated entirely to non-military functions, such as social and educational tasks. This is certainly something very few people outside Israel are aware of, and yet is important in understanding the role of the IDF in Israeli society.

The IDF has been in existence from the declaration of Israel's statehood in 1948. Since then Israel has been engaged in five major conflicts with neighbouring countries as well as the ongoing conflict with the Palestinians. An image that many outside Israel will be familiar with is that of Israeli soldiers at checkpoints and borders in the West Bank and Gaza. But the threat of terrorism ensures that the IDF's extensive role in stopping attacks makes them highly visible within Israel also, everywhere from shopping malls in Tel

Aviv to tourist sites in Jerusalem. As Israel's enemies' tactics have changed, so has the strategy of the IDF in guarding Israeli lives. When you consider the range of duties and functions an Israeli soldier has to carry out, you begin to respect much more the 18- to 21-year-old conscripts who risk their lives for the protection of others, day in and day out.

With this in mind, I reflect on the Israeli soldiers we were privileged enough to meet on the trip. The first members of the IDF we came in contact with were responsible for looking after a section of the security fence near the town of Qalqilya. Though the problems caused by Israel's security fence in restricting the movements of the Palestinian residents of Qalqilya are severe and well known, it was revealing to see the situation from the ordinary Israeli soldier's perspective.

It was amazing to see the technology involved in guarding and protecting only a small section of the fence. It was also enlightening to witness the dedication of the team of soldiers charged with this responsibility. Though I was already aware of the age of the majority of Israeli soldiers, I was still struck to see for myself quite how young some of these men and women looked. Despite this, they were carrying out their duties with commitment and a fastidious attention to detail which is necessary to ensure the fence is not breached.

Each part of the security barrier has a similar team of soldiers based at surveillance centres. Sensors on the fence send back messages to the control centres, and the soldiers have to be constantly alert and ready to visit the fence if any interference is detected. It is an enormous responsibility. With over a thousand Israeli civilians murdered by terrorists since 2000, many by suicide bombers originating from the West Bank, each soldier knows the carnage and destruction that could result if they let their guard slip. The job is dangerous too. Sometimes traps can be set, but despite this the soldiers remain remarkably focused and proud of their work.

Speaking to them allowed us to see for ourselves their dedication and resilience. It was humbling as well. I remember myself as an 18-year-old and cannot believe quite how mature these teenagers are.

Another part of our trip allowed us more contact with Israeli soldiers when we visited an IDF base close to the Lebanese border. We stood barely a hundred metres from a Hezbollah outpost on the other side of the border. There we got more of a sense of how the soldiers live during their time in the army.

We saw the barracks where they sleep, the hall where they eat and the training area where the tanks stand. The cheerful friendliness of the soldiers surprised many on the delegation. But it is more easily understandable if you consider how important a sense of humour is in such circumstances.

As with the team at the fence, despite the lightheartedness of some of the conversation, it was clear how seriously they took their work. Mistakes here can be costly. Even a small error can cost lives. That thought makes you realise quite how difficult a challenge these young people face, especially considering that the officers and commanders are often in their early twenties as well.

Chatting to the soldiers, it is clear that they are not too dissimilar to your average British teenager in their ambitions for the future (often involving university), their taste in music or their general outlook on life. However, their outlook is obviously affected by the situation they, and Israelis more widely, find themselves in.

Today, the IDF faces many nuanced challenges, foremost of which is the task of curbing terrorism. However, they are also charged with enforcing peace arrangements, and if all goes according to plan, they will play a key role in evacuating settlers from the Gaza Strip. Though particular examples of misdemeanours by Israeli soldiers at checkpoints receive widespread media attention, it is noticeable that in many cases Israeli soldiers are aware of the sensitivities of the situation and try and be as unobtrusive as possible to the Palestinians passing them daily. On a day-to-day level, soldiers often try as hard as they can to calm inflamed situations and avoid using force or violence.

It has been said that Israel cannot afford to even lose one war, or one battle. This is understandable given the country's small population, relative isolation in the Middle East, and size (comparable to that of Wales and just nine miles wide at its narrowest point). Since its creation, several aggressive wars have been waged against Israel and her defence force has become one of the world's strongest. But when talking to ordinary Israelis or to the nation's leaders, you feel Israel would rather this was not the case. It would rather its youth didn't have to be conscripted, and that it did not have to ensure it was always one step ahead in the battle for safety and security.

As things are, for many young Israelis their time in the army defines them as young adults. After their compulsory service is completed, many choose to travel, and then go to university. But some conscripts decide to stay on and pursue a career in the armed forces. As a result, the IDF has been, and continues to be, an important source of talent and a training ground for much of Israel's political leadership. This is another reason why, as an institution, the IDF plays a significant role in defining Israel.

The image of the Israeli military in many people's heads is one of tanks. This image immediately unravels when faced with the young men and women, the human face of the IDF, who make up the bulk of the army.

Whilst for most people in Britain, the years from 18 to 21 are those of least responsibility, for Israelis of the same age, life-and-death decisions are placed in their hands on a daily basis. Meeting the soldiers face to face and seeing their experiences at first hand is highly instructive. Some vocal critics of Israel, and particularly of the IDF, might benefit from such an experience. Their criticisms would be met with the difficult reality which faces these soldiers, and Israel, every day.

The Israeli Labor Party: modernisation and renewal

by Paul Richards

The most telling remark for me from the entire trip was made, almost casually, by two Labor Members of the Knesset whom we met, Collette Avital MK and Yuli Tamir MK. They said (and I paraphrase) that the Israeli Labor Party (ILP) had assumed that the priority was security, and with that once gained, the Party could turn its attention to economic development and social progress. Today, after nearly sixty years of war and terrorism, the Israeli Labor Party is recognising that it must fight for peace and for progress, *at the same time.* This essay explores what the ILP may have to go through to become a modernised social democratic party, true to its ideals and history, but in tune with modern Israeli society, and crucially, capable of taking a leading role within government once again.

The constant threat to Israel's peace – the frequent suicide bombings, missile attacks, and wars with its neighbours – have given the Israeli Labor Party a distinct ethos and ideology which distinguish it from its brother and sister Labour and social democratic parties in other democratic states. No other social democratic party has a comparable history. Parties such as the social democratic SPD in Germany, the Parti Socialiste in France, or the Swedish Social Democrats have dealt with world wars, periods of occupation, or outlawing by the state. But the western European socialist and social democrat parties have enjoyed sixty years of peace, economic growth, and for the most part periods in office. Even the social democratic parties of Eastern Europe, such as those in the Czech Republic and Poland, have experienced a decade and a half of democracy, unencumbered by external threats, following the collapse of communism. By contrast, the Israeli Labor Party has had to confront constant threats to the existence of the state.

Amos Oz suggested that the difference between Israeli left and right is merely a question of geography – in other words, the differing positions on borders and territory. But the history of the mainstream left in Israel tells a different story.

The Israeli Labor Party – or Mifleget Ha-Avoda – was created in 1968, but its roots are in parties which governed Israel from 1948 to 1977. Like the UK Labour Party, the Israeli Labor Party is a coalition of socialist groups, anchored in the trade union movement, under the banner of a single party. The backbone of the Labor Party is Mapai, a socialist, pioneering and pragmatic party that was founded in 1930 as a result of the merger of two other parties. Mapai became the main Jewish party before 1948 and contested the extremist and terrorist policies of the ultra-nationalist right wing.

In many ways, the history of the early years of the state of Israel is a history of its labour movement, with its kibbutzim (agricultural communes), moshavim (communal towns), and the dominance of the trade union movement (Histadrut). Visions of workers toiling together in co-operation to reclaim the deserts, build a socialist economy, and create a democratic state were the idealistic images which inspired socialists around the world in the 1940s and 1950s.

Joshua Muravchik's *Heaven on Earth: the Rise and Fall of Socialism* (Encounter Books, San Francisco, 2002) claims that despite the failure of socialism worldwide:

> There was, however, one exception to this unbroken
> record of disappointment. In the biblical promised land,
> the promise of socialism was at last fulfilled.

However, Muravchik charts the undermining of the kibbutz movement by changes in society, rising affluence, and the election of the right-of-centre Likud in 1977, which changed the kibbutzim's beneficial tax breaks. It is telling that as early as 1965, Giles Radice's *Democratic Socialism: a Short Survey* (Longman, London, 1965) stated:

> The universal applicability of Israeli co-operation
> should not, however be exaggerated. Precisely because it
> was as much a political as an economic exercise, Israeli
> co-operation demands a certain degree of political and
> social sophistication; and it is revealing that the relative
> share of the co-operatives in the Israeli economy has
> declined.

One of the key points from our meeting with Knesset

members Collette Avital and Yuli Tamir was that the decline of the kibbutz movement had undermined one of the main props of the Labor Party. The decline of the trade unions and the privatisation of state-owned industry presented a similar psephological problem. The Labor Party is losing its core voters, and has not yet found a way to replace them.

This is a classic social-democratic dilemma. In the UK, the problem for the Labour Party of a declining class base and growing affluence was identified in 1978 by Eric Hobsbawm's 'The Forward March of Labour Halted?' This landmark lecture (later published in *The Forward March of Labour Halted?*, NLB in association with *Marxism Today*, London, 1981) showed that if the Labour Party relied on appeals to trade unionists and the traditional left, based on outdated assumptions about their motivations and culture, Labour would never win enough votes to govern. This premise guided the modernisation of Labour's policies and structures in the 1980s and 1990s. It led to the contest for votes in 'middle England', which Labour emphatically won in 1997.

So the Israeli Labor Party needs to build a new coalition of voters ('middle Israel'?), from new social classes and sections of society, beyond its own traditional heartlands. The method the British Labour Party employed to achieve this was a combination of structural and political renewal. On the structural side, Labour diminished the role of the trade union block vote, in favour of the membership in constituencies. The key events were reforms to the voting system at conference, the National Executive structure, and the introduction of One Member One Vote (OMOV) for parliamentary candidate selections. These reforms were designed to enfranchise the individual members of the party, who historically had been outvoted by trade union block votes, a product of Labour's federal structure. These structural reforms were also symbolic of a party willing to take on vested interests and prepared to modernise itself in the face of changing times and conditions.

The political renewal, which went alongside the structural reforms, was based on a rediscovery of traditional Labour values and their application to modern problems. By placing 'traditional values in a modern setting', Labour could approach modern issues free from dogma and outdated policies, but able to craft convincing solutions. Neil Kinnock's policy review in the late 1980s started the process, but it was Tony Blair's dramatic reworking of Clause IV in 1995 which gave the party a clear, unambiguous ideological framework. Tony Blair argued that the reform of the Labour Party would be a precursor to reform of the country.

The Israeli Labor Party has not gone through any comparable process of soul-searching and recovery. With just nineteen seats in the Knesset, it is at the lowest ebb in its history.

The Israeli Labor Party's problem is a lack of distinctive identity. Its pursuit of peace and security, especially disengagement from the occupied territories and support for the two-state solution, has been usurped by Likud's adoption of similar policies. The discrediting of the Oslo process, with which Labor was so closely associated, by the rise in terrorist violence, has also discredited the party. Perhaps the ILP's most risky move of all is joining the Likud-led coalition government. It was clear from our discussions with Labor members that this development was not without pain and anxiety, especially given Likud's privatisation programme. It would certainly not have come about without an enormous sense of responsibility for ensuring that the Gaza disengagement plan is carried through. In fact, veteran Labor leader Shimon Peres went so far as to say, 'I will not forgive myself if, because of our hesitations over whether to join the government, the disengagement is not implemented.'

It is proof of the unique circumstances of the Israeli Labor Party that forming a government with the right-wing Likud can be conducted without a major split, such as that which befell Labour in the UK in 1929 when Ramsay MacDonald formed the National Government.

There are, of course, signs of hope. In a trendy Tel Aviv bar, we met young men and women from the new guard of the Israeli Labor Party. They respected their party's past, but were not prisoners to it. With new Labor faces in the coalition government, including Ophir Pines-Paz, Isaac Herzog and Shalom Simhon, a new cadre of modernisers is starting to make itself known to the wider electorate.

One rising star, Guy Spigelman, is a relatively recent arrival to Israel from Australia. He is as far from the image of the traditional kibbutznik or member of Histradrut as you can imagine. He works in the IT sector. His grouping, centred on the online magazine *Revival*, recognises that the party has to change to survive. Faced with elections in 2006, Spigelman writes:

Given this timeframe, the Party should now conduct a serious reform process. As so many of our sister parties have shown – the way back to the national leadership starts with fixing our own shop.

The exact nature of this reform process will require serious deliberation and will need to be conducted with great care. But the lesson from Britain and elsewhere is that it is possible for parties of the left, despite huge electoral setbacks, to reform, renew, regroup, and form governments. If reform is guided by principles and values, rather than electoral expediency, and is anchored in the best traditions of openness and democratic debate, there is no reason why Israel's Labor Party cannot catch the mood of the new Israel just as surely as its early leaders, such as David Ben Gurion and Golda Meir, led the State in the past. The trick will be to convince a new generation of voters, for whom Ben Gurion and Meir are ancient history, that Labor is fresh and relevant to their lives. If differing opinions of security are all that is on offer, voters will stick with Likud. If social progress coupled with individual prosperity – for all the citizens of Israel – can be convincingly offered by Labor, then it can win again.

The Middle East reform agenda

by Huw Irranca-Davies MP

The Israel–Palestine conflict has destroyed lives and inflicted prolonged suffering and hardship on Palestinians and Israelis. The $4.5 billion of the Palestinian budget devoured by the second Intifada could have been better invested in poverty alleviation and measures to stimulate economic growth, and the Palestinian unemployment rate has climbed to nearly one third of the population. Israel's relations with many nations, particularly in the Muslim and Arab world, have been tested nearly to destruction.

The emotional and psychological essence of the Israel–Palestine conflict carries the confrontation over into another, more intractable dimension. The State of Israel, founded in the aftermath of one of the darkest chapters of human history, simply cannot allow itself to accept blind hatred of Jews and dumb antisemitism. The Palestinians, on the other hand, cannot be denied their right to put forward their legitimate demands for autonomy and must be allowed to live peacefully in their homeland.

The complexity and severity of the situation has led many observers to regard the wider Middle East region's stability and prosperity as though it were entirely dependent on this one issue alone. Testament to this is the disproportionately high number of initiatives and statements relating to the Middle East – including many originating from the EU and UN – which focus wholly on Israel–Palestine. While this conflict is unarguably crucial to peace in the Middle East and to a better understanding between the Arab world and the West, the dominance it holds over wider issues in the region is both destructive and dangerous.

Let's begin with some truisms: firstly, solving the Israel–Palestine conundrum is of central importance to wider and lasting security, stability and peace in the Middle East; secondly, resolving this thorny issue will help diminish the hostility between Arab and non-Arab, even between Muslim and non-Muslim.

Whilst truisms can provide a useful shorthand to understanding complicated matters, they can also be intellectually lazy and socio-politically hazardous, if they allow us to disregard other painful challenges that confront the region. One of the greatest challenges facing Arab nations is that of democratic reform.

Arab countries sometimes stand accused of having despotic tendencies. Yet the emergence of modern, recognisable democracies in Europe is itself a relatively new phenomenon, and centuries of bloody religious wars under various authoritarian rulers preceded Europe's recent enlightenment. Arab people are no more inclined towards authoritarianism than any other people, and to suggest otherwise is to accept a self-fulfilling prophecy of despair.

In fact, in the 1960s and 1970s many Arab nations experimented with combinations of nationalism and socialism, reflecting a clear strand of global Third World politics at the time, which disappeared along with the Cold War. Back in the 1980s some Arab countries – including Jordan, Egypt and Tunisia – began to move towards multi-party democracy, but this faltering start quickly unravelled.

Now, twenty years later, the early shoots of democratic reform are reappearing. This is largely due to simmering public dissatisfaction in many Arab nations with corruption and socio-economic inequalities, but is also thanks to quiet international diplomacy and – it cannot be ignored – the deposing of Saddam Hussein and subsequent elections in Iraq.

Most Arab nations now have a fragile cadre of progressive, liberal voices who want democratic reform, human rights and freedom of expression. But these voices are frequently confronted by reactionary elements that instinctively seek to entrench authoritarian rule. The progressives want to engage with the international community, including Israel, but are relatively powerless in comparison with the recidivist tendency that is overtly hostile to western values, and to the very existence of Israel.

The challenge that this hostility poses for progressive Arab nations and leaders, let alone for those leaders reluctant to confront radical political forces inside their own country, is formidable. However, this challenge must be met.

Egypt's 'national dialogue', instigated by President Hosni Mubarak, is a good example of cautious reform taking place. The ruling National Democratic Party plans to engage opposition parties and politicians in discussions on political reform ahead of the planned elections. This 'bottom-up' reform should be applauded and quietly encouraged by international observers. Nonetheless, political opponents and government critics in Egypt are still exposed to intimidation and harassment, and the Egyptian authorities habitually defy international opinion by arresting alleged political opponents for extended periods of pre-trial detention. These violations of human rights need to be addressed unambiguously, as they sit uncomfortably with Egypt's reform agenda.

Saudi Arabia's first nationwide municipal elections were a hopeful sign in the kingdom, and even though women were not allowed to vote, there are encouraging signals in this direction. Yet there is still a long way to go in Saudi Arabia, in terms of both human rights generally, and women's rights specifically.

Numerous reports of harassment, arrests, unfair trials, imprisonment and travelling restrictions on human rights defenders and human rights activists still emanate from Syria. The Foreign Secretary rightly called for Syrian troops to be withdrawn from Lebanon. As international pressure is mounting on Damascus, it remains to be seen if Syria can avoid being treated as a 'pariah state'. To achieve this, Syria has to be open to reform, even if it is implemented in a protracted and incremental fashion.

The governments of the Gulf Cooperation Council (GCC) – Bahrain, Kuwait, Oman, Qatar, Saudi Arabia and the United Arab Emirates (UAE) – are frequently criticised by human rights groups for the violence and discrimination against women in their countries.

In short, where undemocratic regimes across the region

disregard human rights, they should not use the Palestinian cause as an excuse for their own misdemeanours.

The elections in Iraq exceeded many expectations. Iraqis cast their votes despite continuing incidents of violence as polling day came and went. However, the lawlessness and increased killings, abductions and rapes that have followed the ousting of Saddam Hussein and the barbarous Baathist regime still present many obstacles for the majority of Iraqis who want to build a stable, peaceful and democratic state. Yet there are many positive indications that this fledgling democracy is healthy, is not deteriorating into factionalism, and is maintaining a focus on improvements to the lives of the Iraqi people rather than the Iraqi elite – a clear break from the past.

The Lebanese Druze leader Walid Jumblatt, who reportedly once rejoiced in the deaths of Israeli soldiers, and of US soldiers in Iraq, recently told the *Washington Post*:

> I was cynical about Iraq, but when I saw the Iraqi people voting three weeks ago, eight million of them, it was the start of a new Arab world ... the Syrian people, the Egyptian people, all say that something is changing. The Berlin Wall has fallen. We can see it.

Israel can be a convenient scapegoat for Arab nations in excusing their failure to deliver Arab people their basic human rights, freedom of speech and the levers of political power. But women in Kuwait were never denied the vote because of the 'Zionist threat', and progress towards democracy and prosperity in Arab nations does not have to wait for a viable and secure Palestinian state. Israel does not stand in the way of reform in the Arab world: Israel and the wider international community would welcome such reform.

Some commentators fear that militant Islamists will hijack any move towards democracy in the Middle East for their own purposes, entering elections simply to subvert the process and impose strict religious rule on the region. They fear this would destroy once and for all the necessary separation of the secular and the religious in the rule of the state. However, Islamic parties and candidates standing in eight Arab countries in the last ten years – Kuwait, Lebanon, Egypt, Jordan, Morocco, Bahrain, Yemen and Algeria – have achieved nothing more than modest results. So, while these experiments in democracy may be fragile, and while there is far to progress with human rights, there has been no dangerous regression to fundamentalist restrictions on freedoms.

However, the road to democracy is extremely dangerous. The process of democratisation, particularly in its early stages, creates instability and the opportunity for conflict or, perversely, usurpation by dictatorial elites. This has been true of the tortuous development of democracy in Europe and the West and is a comment on the process, not the participants. The pace of change must be measured, but the direction clear. The potential prizes of personal liberty, human rights, and socio-economic equality are worth the chase.

Just as the Arab people will be the prime actors in the democratisation of the Arab nations, so the solution to the challenges of Israel and Palestine will ultimately come from the Israelis and Palestinians themselves. Both will require support from international friends, but both hold their destiny in their own hands.

The pressure for long-term reform must come from within, reflecting the culture and priorities of the region: but reform there must be. The Palestinian Authority has set a fine example with democratic renewal of itself, electing a leadership with public support and public accountability, and making a concerted effort to tackle corruption and internal terrorism. This has coincided with a dramatic and positive change of tone in referring to the West and Israel in official media. This signifies a clear willingness to challenge antisemitism, and in so doing, to work towards greater mutual understanding and a peaceful accord among the people of the region.

The dangers of democratic imperialism are all too obvious, and the temptation to promote our particular western mould of democracy among the nations of the Middle East should be guarded against, as should our inclination to demand democratisation overnight. Our western democratic systems have grown incrementally and often painfully over many centuries, so why should we expect others to materialise instantaneously?

A true friend to Israel and the Palestinians, but also to the wider Arab world, must be able to speak frankly and critically, but also constructively. Friends should accept that the Arab nations will not become fully functioning democratic systems overnight. But friends must constantly encourage political and democratic reform.

In conclusion, to focus entirely on the Israel–Palestine

issue to the exclusion of the wider need for the development of democracy is to betray the rights of Arab people throughout the Middle East, and no genuine friend would do this. False friends will continue to speak only of Israel, and make sympathetic noises to the Arab people about the Palestinians. Genuine friends will also be encouraging democratic reform in the region as an equal priority.

Seeing Israel and the Palestinian Territories for the first time

by Tony Young

There have been a number of opportunities for me to visit Israel, but for one reason or another, with pressures of work and family, these chances were never taken. This time it felt right and opportune, as progress towards peace, however fragile, seemed possible.

If, like me, you are born a Jew, although in my case a non-practising one, you cannot ignore your roots. As someone with an interest in history, the opportunity to see Israel and Palestine, to hear first hand the views of both sides in the Middle East conflict, made a visit very worthwhile. The reaction of some colleagues and friends was interesting. Some raised the question of security. My reaction was to respond that these days, wherever you go, travel carries an element of risk. A previous trip to China, for example, coincided with an outbreak of SARS.

As to the nature of the visit, would it be impartial? Would I get to hear a variety of views, both Israeli and Palestinian? The answer was to point to the programme, which included a day in Ramallah and the opportunity to meet Palestinians.

We were a large delegation, nearly thirty in all, including MPs, parliamentary staff and myself, and it was a demanding week of contrasting viewpoints.

Though based in Tel Aviv, the first part of our trip took us on the road to Jerusalem. The history of violence is unavoidable, and our guide pointed to a number of sites in Tel Aviv and Jerusalem that had been the targets of suicide bombers, describing both the social and political impact this had on Israeli society.

The spiritual significance of the country is also immediately striking. Whatever your beliefs, you cannot fail to be impressed by Jerusalem: a concentration of history and diverse cultures that is overwhelming. Wandering through the Old City with all its religious and historical associations, you begin to understand why it has become such a battleground, with every part, however small, hotly disputed.

My first sight of the Western Wall and the Temple Mount, sites of great importance for Muslims and Jews, was awe-inspiring. The importance of the Old City for Christians is also apparent when travelling the route Christ took, marked by the Stations of the Cross. Our visit also took us via a somewhat controversial tunnel, through which you can now walk along the whole of the Western Wall of the temple, built in the reign of King Herod.

Our tour culminated at the Church of the Holy Sepulchre, a site where every inch of space and each artefact is fiercely contested by many branches of the Christian religion. The display of intense rivalry between different faiths, even within the same religion, for me detracted from what should have been a moving experience.

Driving through Tel Aviv and walking through Jerusalem, I got a sense of Israel as experienced by its residents. But as a newcomer to Israel and its politics, it was through hearing at first-hand what officials in the Israeli Ministry of Foreign Affairs had to say that I gained a valuable insight into Israeli government thinking.

There is no doubt that the latest developments in Israel and the Palestinian Territories have created a real opportunity for progress towards peace. But Sharon's brave decision to implement a policy of withdrawal from Gaza and other settlements has brought an inevitable response from hard-line settlers. We saw for ourselves an encampment of thousands of settlers and supporters outside the Knesset on a daily basis. But it is also clear that Sharon has overwhelming public support. This move is evidently part of a strategy that, out of necessity, places a premium on the reduction of terror and improvement of security.

In addition, the security barrier – which Israelis are keen to point out is 95 per cent fence – is a key part of the strategy and has helped greatly to reduce the incidence of suicide bombings. But the reaction on the Palestinian front has been a significant increase in rocket attacks from Gaza. There was a real concern on the part of Israelis that the range of rockets could increase to target larger towns. On a broader strategic level, it is clear that the recent announcement of Russian arms sales to Syria is viewed with concern, as is the implication of Iran in the possible acquisition of nuclear weapons.

However, there is also cautious welcome for the new situation that has been created with the death of Arafat and the election of Mahmoud Abbas. Among Israeli politicians there is a range of views on Abbas. But whatever the view, Israel expects him to demonstrate progress in controlling Palestinian factions who are responsible for terror attacks, against the background of positive steps by Israel to remove settlers.

The next day we travelled, via strongly fortified check points, to Ramallah to engage with members of the Palestinian Authority and Legislative Council. It was important to hear first hand the Palestinian perspective. In our meeting with Qadurra Faris, the then Minister without Portfolio, he expressed his view that a small window of hope had opened in the Palestinian community because of the democratic election of Abbas, who he assured us was extremely serious about negotiations to achieve peace.

However, he stated that Abbas faced problems meeting demands to take control of Palestinian society because Israel had largely destroyed the Palestinian Authority's security infrastructure. He stressed that with Israeli help and co-operation, Abbas would try to achieve a ceasefire, but there had to be an end to Israel's policy of assassinations.

The Minister was challenged on a number of issues, including the Palestinian education system, in which parts of the curriculum portray Israel as the enemy, reducing chances of reconciliation. He suggested that UNESCO could play a role in assessing education in both Israel and Palestine.

Meeting later with the speaker of the Palestinian Legislative Council, Rawhi Fattouh, we were given a further insight into the Palestinian position. He stated that they were against terror attacks on Israeli citizens inside Israel, but stated that the wall would prevent the creation of a Palestinian state. He expressed his belief that if it was purely for security, it could have been built on the Israeli border. And he accused the Israeli army of terrorism, speaking of schoolchildren who have been shot by Israeli snipers.

In the informal atmosphere of a lunch, we had the opportunity to speak to a number of other Palestinian politicians and also to hear of the work being done by the UK to help improve the situation. The British Deputy Consul, Piers Cazalet, briefed us on the work being done to help Palestinians develop security apparatus and the preparatory work for the London meeting on 1 March 2005.

Though our time spent in the Palestinian Territories was all too short, it was an enlightening and memorable experience. The close quarters at which Israeli and Palestinian politicians live and work, in this small piece of land, was brought home to me by the short journey from the Palestinian Interior Ministry in Ramallah to the Israeli Knesset in Jerusalem.

Politics, like life, is unpredictable. A year ago we would have dismissed a Likud–Labor coalition as highly unlikely. Though at the time of our visit it had become a reality, it is clearly a difficult partnership and there are many differences. These include disagreements over how to handle talks with Abbas, especially when responding to incidents of terrorism. The Israeli policy-makers are on the horns of a dilemma. They need to give Abbas an opportunity to control the violent factions in Palestinian society, but he needs to demonstrate real progress in reducing terror.

Speaking to ordinary Members of the Knesset, one is reminded of political issues more familiar from our own political scene. The relationship between Israeli Labor and the Histadrut (the Israeli trade union movement), for example, was an issue of concern to Labor MKs. It became clear that there has been a rift between Histadrut and the Labor Party. The good news is that reconciliation is gathering pace.

It is impossible to get a sense of a country just by meeting politicians. But in a short space of time we also saw an incredible amount of the land itself. Travelling to the Sea of Galilee on the way to viewing the Lebanese border left me with indelible memories. I am grateful for such an enlightening and enjoyable experience, and whilst recognising there are huge problems to be resolved on the way to permanent peace, I was left with a real sense of optimism.

Afterword:
Beyond the headlines

by Meg Munn MP

Just what is it like in Israel and Palestine? Articles in the British media often sum up the situation with a few points – political shifts, conflict, death. Visiting the area shows just how superficial that level of reporting is. In a region where peoples with proud histories are locked in dispute, there is more complexity than the headlines allow.

At our pre-visit briefing in Westminster the week before we went, Ivan Lewis said, 'This is a very interesting time to be visiting the area. A sentence that could have been uttered any time over the last two thousand years.'

Members of the delegation, the largest that Labour Friends of Israel (LFI) have ever sent, were to find out just how true that statement was. Their contributions in this publication illustrate just some of the 'interesting complexities'.

This visit was my second; the first visit was in June 2003, just as a ceasefire had been agreed. That week gave us hope. Leaders from both communities were seeking peace and learning how to trust each other. We also saw some of the bitterness, and at times hatred, held by many. I feared that the injustice and violence would override the desire for peace. Six weeks after the visit, on 19 August 2003, a suicide bomber blew up a bus in Jerusalem, bringing that brief interlude to an end.

Returning eighteen months later, the events of the previous few weeks again gave us hope. The death of Yasser Arafat had not led to civil war or unrest in the Occupied Territories. The election of Mahmoud Abbas as President of the Palestinian Authority had begun a process tinged with possibilities. The ceasefire announced by Abbas and Ariel Sharon, followed by the Israeli cabinet approval of the withdrawal of Jewish settlers and army from Gaza, allowed for guarded optimism.

During our visit, senior members of the Israeli National Security Council and the Israel Defence Forces, including the architect of the Gaza withdrawal plan, expressed their conviction that security will bring peace. Improved security – chiefly the security fence and the cessation of the armed struggle in the Occupied Territories – will, they believe, allow trust to build up between the communities. We have to deal with the realities of the security fence and not be distracted by theoretical positions of those living far away from the situation on the ground.

Visiting the Occupied Territories lays bare the reality of Palestinian life, and the economic cost of the current situation. Travelling from Israel to Ramallah is truly going from a first world country to a developing one. The process of crossing the checkpoint was quicker and less difficult than on my first visit, but the feeling of being penned in is the same. I spoke at length with Dalal Salameh, a member of the Palestinian Authority in Nablus. She told me she has to leave Ramallah by a deadline in order to be able to return to

Nablus before the checkpoint closes. Her top priority was to end this restriction and for Palestinians to be able to move freely in their own land.

On my first visit I was surprised by the size of Ramallah, and the contrasts within it. Some houses would not look out of place in well-off areas in any of our cities in the UK, while in other parts the poverty is only too obvious. The economy has improved over the last eighteen months, and this was noticeable as we travelled. But the posters on the walls spoke of more important change. Eighteen months earlier, the walls had been plastered with posters of suicide bombers and those killed by Israeli incursions. These were almost absent this time. Instead the posters were recognisably about the recent elections for Palestinian President.

Gerald Steinberg, an academic we met from Bar Ilan University, warned against believing that there are easy answers to the problems of the conflict, and that projects of reconciliation are too small to make a difference. However, if we are concerned about the circumstances which breed terrorists, we should support those projects that seek better understanding between the two communities. Children at integrated schools show us that hope for the future need not remain just a dream. These projects search for better ways of living, raising the next generation to understand each other. Small projects they may be, but the Hand-in-Hand project has Jewish parents sending their children to a school in an Arab village in Kfar Kara, a sign for the future.

Our time spent at the Knesset highlighted the importance of the new Israeli national unity government. This development has received less attention than the election of the

Palestinian President, but is no less important to the peace process. Israeli Labor Party politicians accepted that entering a coalition government with Ariel Sharon was risky. While we were at the Knesset, hundreds of young people were demonstrating outside against the possibility of Gaza withdrawal. It was extraordinary to see Ariel Sharon effectively forgoing the support of significant numbers of his party in order to form a government of national unity to complete disengagement.

There are more positive signs now than there have been for some time, but it's a fragile process. Isaac Herzog, Israeli MK and now cabinet minister for housing, told me some months ago that he believed a successful Israeli withdrawal from Gaza and handover to the Palestinian Authority would signal unstoppable progress towards the two-state solution. There will be many challenges in the next few months.

Every decision and every step in Israel carries such implications for the peoples of a land that has lived with conflict for more than fifty years. On returning to the UK, for the first few hours everything seems so ordinary again. But it is this ordinariness that Israelis and Palestinians desire.

Five days on an LFI visit feels like three weeks – there is so much to see, absorb and learn. The security arrangements that are commonplace; the young soldiers who are so much younger than even the youngest of our delegation; standing on the border with Lebanon and knowing that they are being watched by Hezbollah. All this in a beautiful land – it's hard to imagine anywhere more peaceful than the Sea of Galilee.

There will be obstacles along the way; groups within both communities who do not support this process and will use violence to try and stop it. Support and encouragement by the international community could not be more important. Inevitably we compare this peace process to our own situation in Northern Ireland. Despite the halting progress, we are thankfully a long way removed from the regular violence that has taken so many lives. Everyone we met in Israel and Palestine agreed that they have to keep trying to move forward. There is no other option than to continue to seek peace.

About the contributors

Luke Akehurst was the Labour parliamentary candidate for Castle Point in 2005. He was parliamentary candidate for Aldershot in 2001 and is Labour Chief Whip on Hackney Council. A former National Secretary of Labour Students, he works as an Associate Director at Weber Shandwick Public Affairs, specialising in defence issues.

Jennifer Gerber is Deputy Director of Progress and also works for Andy Burnham MP. Previously she has worked for the Labour Party. Jennifer is a keen writer on the Middle East and antisemitism.

Huw Irranca-Davies is the Labour Member of Parliament for Ogmore, South Wales. He has visited the Middle East on several occasions.

Dr Ashok Kumar was elected as Labour Member of Parliament for Middlesbrough South and East Cleveland in the 1997 general election. During his career as a research scientist for British Steel he built his local reputation as a councillor, and now as an MP he is committed to fighting injustice in Teesside. Of his many parliamentary interests, the Middle East is one about which he feels particularly passionate.

Ivan Lewis is Labour Member of Parliament for Bury South, and Economic Secretary to the Treasury. He is a former Vice-Chair of Labour Friends of Israel and a Trustee of the Holocaust Educational Trust.

Meg Munn was elected Labour Member of Parliament for Sheffield Heeley in 2001. She was previously Assistant Director for Children's Services at City of York Council. She is currently the Deputy Minister for Women and Equality, and Chair of the Co-operative Group of MPs.

Linda Perham was an active member of Labour Friends of Israel during her time as Labour Member of Parliament for Ilford South, from 1997 to 2005. She served on the parliamentary executive of LFI and also as the Secretary of the British–Israel Group.

Rachel Reeves works as an economist in London, and has studied economics at Oxford, Harvard and the London School of Economics. Rachel was Labour's parliamentary candidate in Bromley and Chislehurst in the 2005 general election.

Paul Richards is a member of the Fabian Society executive, and works part-time for Hazel Blears MP. He is the author of several books and pamphlets, including *The Case for Socialism, How to Win an Election,* and *Is the Party Over?* He is the editor of *Tony Blair in His Own Words.*

Siôn Simon is the Labour Member of Parliament for Birmingham, Erdington. He was formerly Associate Editor of the *Spectator* and a columnist on the *Daily Telegraph*, the *News of the World*, the *Daily Express* and many other publications.

Tony Young (Lord Young of Norwood Green) was raised to the peerage in 2004, having served as Joint General Secretary of the Communication Workers Union, President of the Trade Union Congress, and Governor of the BBC. He is currently Chairman of One World Broadcasting Trust.

Index